She Kept Dancing

The True Story of a Professional Dancer with a Limb Difference

Written by SYDNEY MESHER and CATHERINE LAUDONE

Illustrated by NATELLE QUEK

Feiwel and Friends · New York

Sydney was born with ten toes and five fingers. But it was her toes that Mom noticed first. "I can tell she's going to be a dancer," Mom told Dad.

And it turned out Mom was right! Before she
even crawled, Sydney was twirling, swaying,
and leaping around the house.

When her parents saw how much joy dancing brought Sydney, they
enrolled her in dance class. On her first day, Sydney was so excited.
It felt like tap dancers were rat-a-tat-tatting through her whole body.

But when she walked into the studio, some of the kids grew quiet. Others called her a monster when they saw she had one hand instead of two.

Sydney's sadness was a slow dance with many
turns and sweeping gestures.

After class, she told Mom what had happened.

"Those kids have never met anyone with a limb difference before,"
Mom said. "And sometimes people are unkind when they meet someone
new or different. But don't let their mean words keep you from doing
what you love. Keep dancing."

So Sydney did. She kept dancing at the next class, and the next, and the next, until her classmates finally started seeing her as just another dancer.

But when Sydney walked into kindergarten for the first time, it was like the first day of dance class all over again.

Sydney's heart slipped and fell to the floor. *Will it always be like this?* she wondered.

But she remembered what Mom had told her, and so she picked her heart back up and kept dancing through the day.

A few months later, Sydney was offered the chance to try out a prosthetic hand. It attached to her arm, except she wouldn't be able to move the fingers.

When she wore it, bullies started calling her "the girl with the fake hand." Sydney did her best to ignore them—she wanted to make her decision based on what felt right to her and not what other people thought.

After a few days, Sydney decided she felt more like herself without the prosthetic. Her self-confidence was a wild freestyle number.

As Sydney grew older, dancing continued to be the one thing that always made her feel good about herself.

No two dances were the same. Each one was beautiful because it was different—just like how Sydney's body was beautiful because it was different.

Sydney found that she could say more with her body than she ever could with words.

She soaked up every tap, ballet, jazz, and hip-hop lesson offered at her local studio.

And when she ran out of dance classes to take there, she enrolled in a performing arts high school, where she learned new ways to swing, shake, stomp, flap-shuffle-flap, twist, and twirl.

Sydney kept dancing all through high school, past graduation, and across state lines until she landed in New York City.

On the way to her college dorm, she passed by Radio City Music Hall, where the famous Radio City Rockettes danced. The Rockettes were some of the best dancers in the world.

RADIO CITY MUSIC HALL

RADIO CITY MUSIC HALL

Will I be good enough to dance there one day? Sydney wondered. She decided that she would practice even harder to make her wish of dancing on that stage come true.

Sydney still saw people whispering and stealing glances at her when she walked into open auditions, but it only made her more determined to become the best dancer she could possibly be. No one would ever say that she had gotten a dancing job out of pity for her limb difference.

All of Sydney's hard work paid off when she landed her first big job as one of the first-ever women backup dancers for BTS, a popular South Korean boy band. She would perform with them for their one-night-only show in New York.

As the concert began, her heart pounded a thunderous beat in her chest. *Am I really good enough to be up here?* she worried. *What if I make a mistake in front of such a big audience?*

Sydney danced over her doubts and onto the stage. She kept dancing and dancing, and with each step, she became as powerful and fierce as a lioness. Up there, she was no longer Sydney the dancer with a limb difference. She was just Sydney the dancer. And that was good enough for her.

After that night, Sydney felt unstoppable, like a train going full speed!

She kept dancing and dancing until . . .

. . . she couldn't dance anymore.

Having a broken foot was tough enough, but using crutches with only one hand was painful and sometimes nearly impossible. For the first time in her life, Sydney truly felt held back by her limb difference.

Without dance, it felt like she had lost her voice. She didn't even know how to tell others just how sad and angry she felt.

While she was recovering, Sydney began to notice movement in unexpected places, like on the city streets outside her window.

She saw people dashing, tugging, stopping—no, *pausing*.

As if holding a pose in a group dance and waiting for the right beat to jump back in.

That's when she realized that her injury was just a pause. An intermission.

Hope leaped inside Sydney's heart. Her dancing days were far from over.

After healing from her injury, Sydney graduated from college with a degree in dance.

She started taking on different jobs and was surprised to find some of them required her to model and act more than dance.

She glided down the runway at New York City's Fashion Week and posed for photo shoots.

She step-stomp-stepped at a music festival and starred in a commercial.

With every new job, she hoped someone else with a limb difference would see her and know that their own body was beautiful, too, and worth celebrating.

Sydney's first love was dance, though, and she had a secret wish: She still wanted to be a Radio City Rockette, to dance with the best of the best in a grand theater.

She'd auditioned for the Rockettes a few times over the years but had never made the cut. But Sydney just had to try
one
more
time.

Walking into the audition, Sydney felt more confident than she ever had before. She didn't notice if anyone was staring or whispering—she was solely focused on giving the best performance of her life.

When it was her turn, Sydney kicked high and kept her lines ruler-straight.

She swung her arms and shook her shoulders. She tap-tap-tapped and flap-flap-shuffle-flapped. Then she struck a pose and smiled, holding perfectly still.

In that moment, Sydney's feelings of pure joy and pride shimmied from the top of her head all the way down to her long toes. No matter what the outcome, she knew she'd danced her best, and that was good enough for her. And this time . . .

. . . she did it!

Sydney was the first Rockette in history with a visible disability, and people came from all over the world to watch her and the other Rockettes perform in the Radio City Christmas Spectacular.

Dancing in the colorful costumes on the big stage under the dazzling lights was more wonderful than Sydney had ever dared to dream.

And best of all, each show was an opportunity for Sydney to share her message of celebrating different body types using a language everyone could understand: dance.

After the curtain fell at the end of each show, Sydney often met backstage with children from the audience who had limb differences of their own. Sydney always made sure to reassure them, saying, "You can do everything that you put your mind to."

When everyone had left, Sydney would sometimes pause before heading home. She'd look out at the music hall, remembering the soaring music and running through the choreography again in her mind.

I still can't believe that I get to come to work here every day and do what I love, she would think. *I can't imagine what my life would be like if I hadn't kept dancing.*

Her joy was a mash-up of dance styles: a pirouette twirling
into a jazz swing before tapping into fast hip-hop steps.
It was one of a kind. Just like her.

A Note from Sydney:

My mother knew I was going to be a dancer, because when I was born, she noticed I had long toes. To her, that was a sign that I was an artist. Apparently it was evident to everyone—even before I knew—that my purpose was to create.

My journey with art has flowed in the most extraordinary ways, though my heart always pulls me back to dance. My desire for movement in harmonious collaboration with music will always make me feel the most alive. Every day, I am thankful to be in an industry and a time that allows creation and individuality. Within this is the acceptance of disabilities.

My sources for inspiration were limited when I was growing up. I did not have the same ability to research people like me as most kids do today. My family relied on a small selection of picture books, newspaper articles, and others' personal stories to help me feel included and normal. As a child, picture books resonated with me because I could visualize the story and the characters. So when it came time to choose a format for sharing my own story, there was no question that it had to be a picture book.

Creating this book—my book—is the most humbling yet important act I could do in my career. I hope that you can see my story and begin to dream of creating yours, too. And I hope everyone gets the same chance I've had to live out their dreams.

For my family, for letting me dance through dinner

—S. M.

For Mom & Dad—thank you for always believing in me

—C. L.

For Yvonne and Kevin

—N. Q.

A Feiwel and Friends Book
An imprint of Macmillan Publishing Group, LLC
120 Broadway, New York, NY 10271 · mackids.com

Our books may be purchased in bulk for promotional, educational, or business use. Please contact your local bookseller or the Macmillan Corporate
and Premium Sales Department at (800) 221-7945 ext. 5442 or by email at MacmillanSpecialMarkets@macmillan.com.

Library of Congress Control Number: 2022949547

First edition, 2023
Art directed by Sharismar Rodriguez and designed by Elynn Cohen.
Artwork rendered digitally with Procreate and Photoshop
Feiwel and Friends logo designed by Filomena Tuosto
Printed in China by RR Donnelley Asia Printing Solutions Ltd., Dongguan City, Guangdong Province
ISBN 978-1-250-84267-1 (hardcover)
1 3 5 7 9 10 8 6 4 2